Published 1973 by The Hamlyn Publishing Group Limited
London · New York · Sydney · Toronto
Astonaut House, Feltham, Middlesex, England

Title of the original edition *Vive les Saisons*

Printed in England by C. Tinling & Co. Limited
ISBN 0 600 36557 3

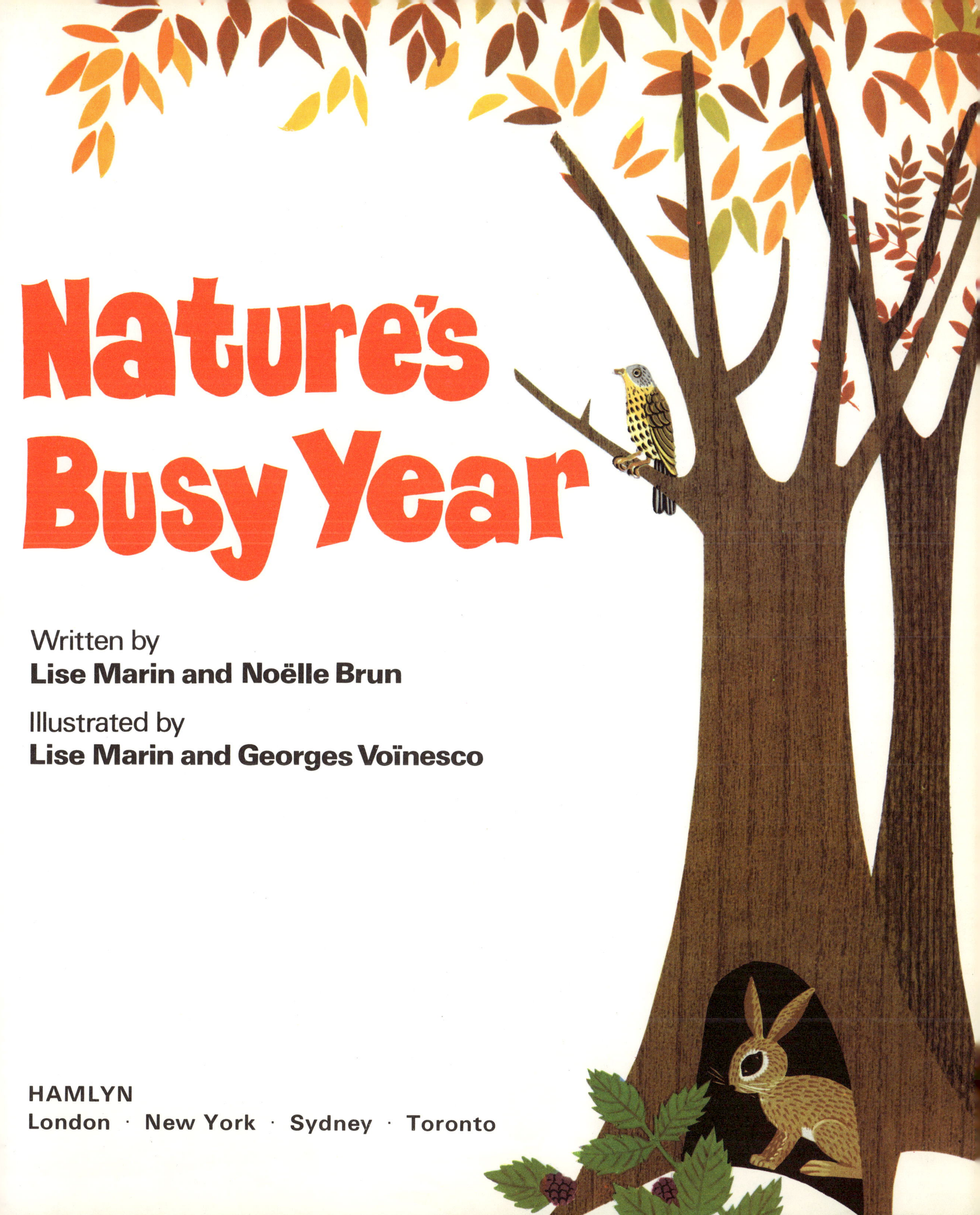

Nature's Busy Year

Written by
Lise Marin and Noëlle Brun

Illustrated by
Lise Marin and Georges Voïnesco

HAMLYN
London · New York · Sydney · Toronto

Spring
The buds you see on the ends of branches are the first sign of spring.
Plants pop out of the ground and grow in the sunlight.
The pretty snowdrops are the first flowers of the year.
If you put a bean seed in a pot filled with soil . . .
before long, a shoot will appear.
IN SPRINGTIME, PEOPLE ARE
As it grows, the shoot will push the seed out of the ground and the bean plant will grow out of this seed.

cuckoo
Swallows return home
from hot countries.
BUSY SOWING SEEDS
butterfly
Birds build their
nests and rabbits
come out of their
burrows to explore.
As for the cuckoo, it is
busy laying its eggs
in other birds' nests . . .

In winter, nature sleeps, in spring, she awakens.

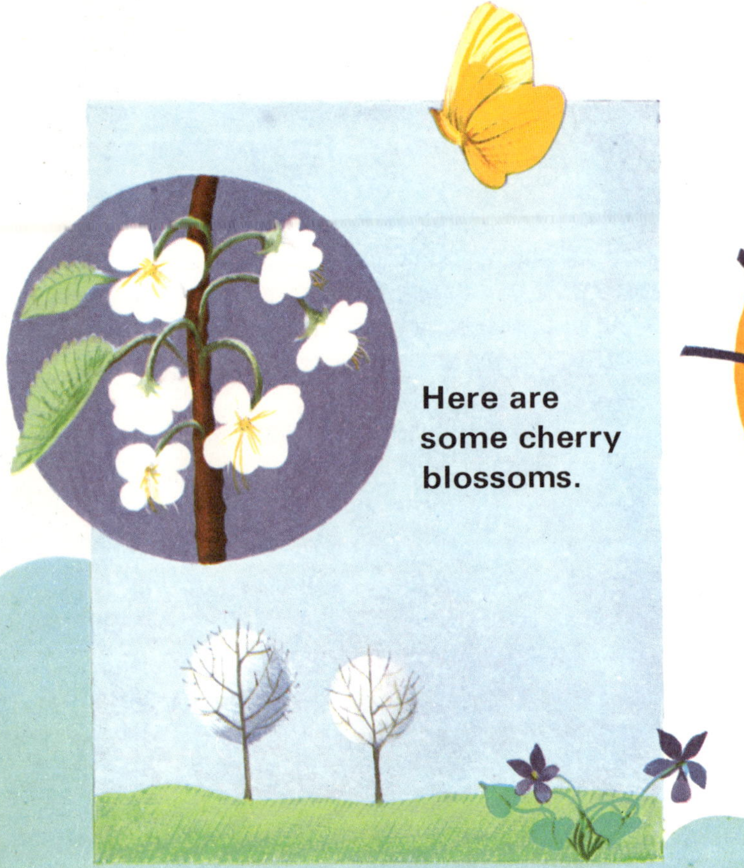
Here are
some cherry
blossoms.

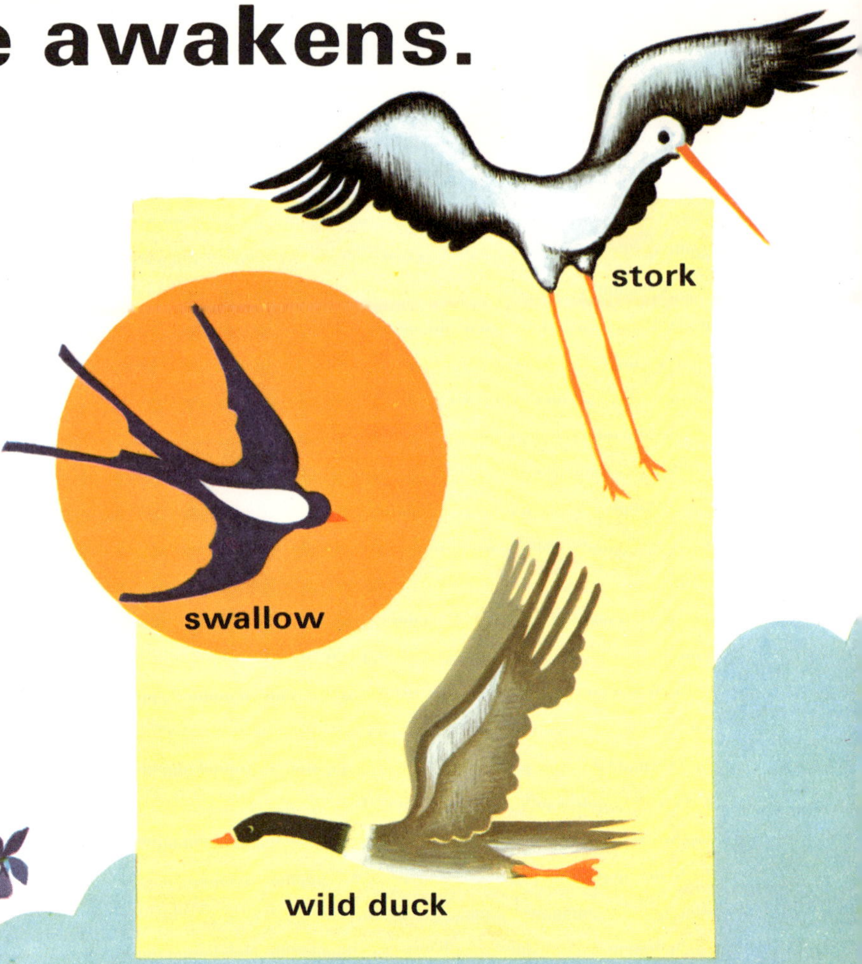
stork
swallow
wild duck

When the blossoms on the trees have faded, they change into fruit.

These birds are migratory which means they go away in the winter and return home in the spring.

During our walks in the garden or in the country, we meet all sorts of little creatures.

butterfly
snail
lizard
bumblebee
frog

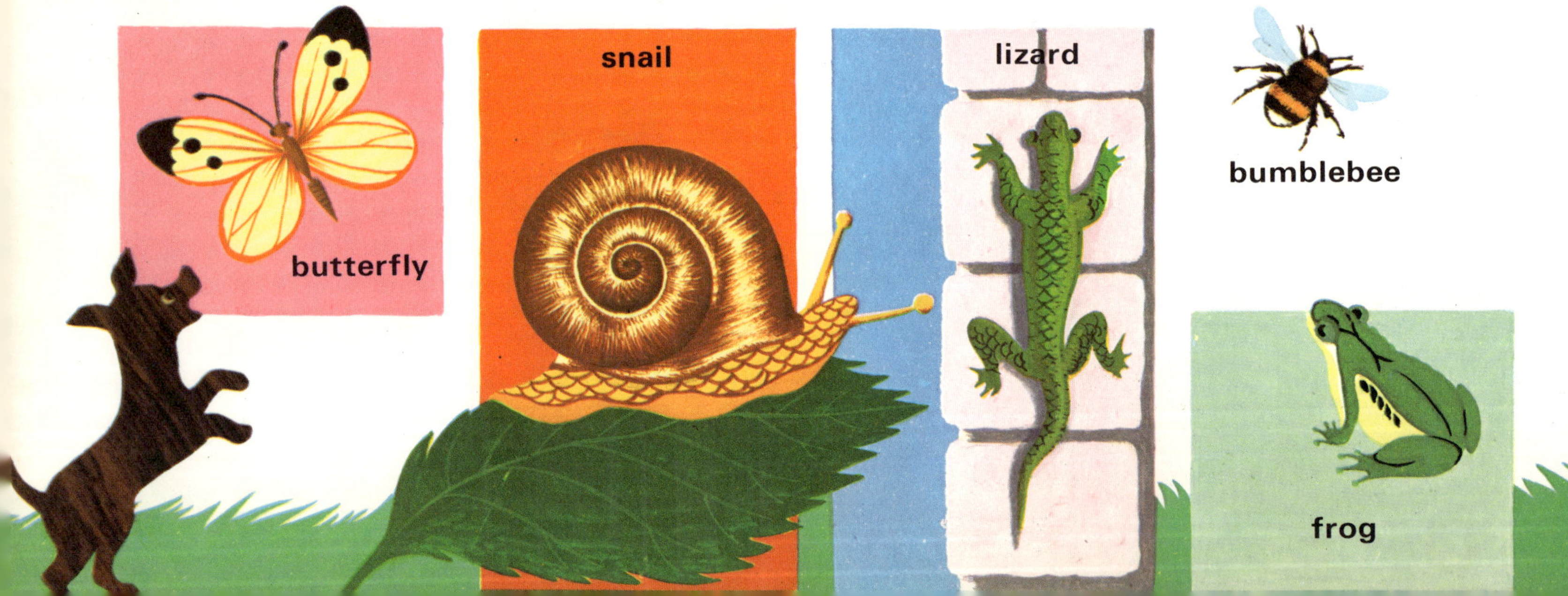

The bluetit makes a nest of twigs in which to lay its eggs.

Twenty-one days after a hen first lays an egg and sits on it, a chick hatches.

In spring the grass starts to grow again. We have to mow it so that the lawn stays green and nice.

This is also the time to prune shrubs.

In the country, we can pick pretty flowers

To make a spring bouquet:

1. Put a pin-holder in a vase. Place some mauve irises in it.

2. Then put in some jonquils, buttercups and wallflowers.

3. Add a few white irises and some blue primulas.

4. Put violets and lilies-of-the-valley around the base.

Here are some pretty leaves:

To make a collection of dried flowers:

Put a flower on a piece of blotting paper.

Cover it with another piece of blotting paper.

Now place the flowers and blotting paper under a heavy book.

A few days later, the flower will be dry. Now you can tape it in a scrapbook with other dried flowers.

The tiny world of birds and insects

Here and there butterflies fly happily.

Bees go from flower to flower to gather the pollen from which they make honey.

During the spring, green and all the other colours of nature are at their softest.

Happy Easter!

Ding-dong! Ding-dong!
The bells gaily ring.
Easter has arrived.
But where does the custom of
Easter eggs come from?

It comes from long ago, when it was forbidden to eat eggs during Lent.
To celebrate the end of Lent, everyone ate more eggs than ever.
Soon people began making chocolate eggs.

Excited children look for eggs hidden in gardens and houses.

How to dye and decorate your eggs:

Dilute some dye according to the maker's instructions.

Then plunge hard-boiled eggs into the coloured water.

After taking the eggs out of the dye, let them dry naturally. Now you can paint them with interesting patterns or faces.

April in the country

There are many things to see in the country in April . . . A farmer ploughs his field with his tractor. The farm animals enjoy eating the fresh grass, insects and little worms. Wild birds move about without fear, for hunting is not allowed in the spring.

Why do people play practical jokes, or 'April fool jokes', on the 1st April?

Because 400 years ago, a king decided that the first day of the year would be 1st January and not 1st April as it had been up until then. Since, we have celebrated the New Year on 1st January but we still enjoy playing practical jokes to celebrate 1st April.

Two useful gifts

To make this pretty bookmark, cut a piece of coloured cardboard 4 cm wide × 22 cm deep. Cut one of the ends into a point. Using bright colours, paint on flower pictures and leaves.

This simple decorative folder will keep your papers in order.
Take a piece of coloured cardboard 24 cm deep × 42 cm wide.
First fold this in half and then fold the left and right sides into the inside along a line 5 cm from each edge. Paste these two bands at the top and at the bottom. Decorate the folder with a dried flower.

You now have two super but useful items to keep and use yourself or to give as gifts.

The sun shines more often in spring than in winter . . . but it also rains.

The rain helps the thirsty plants to grow so the rain in spring is very important.

After the rain the sun shines again and our games in the fresh air will be livelier than ever.

Summer

Cock-a-doodle-doo!

The sun rises early! The day begins at five o'clock in the morning and ends at about nine o'clock, then, little by little, the days get shorter.

THE BEGINNING OF SUMMER

What is the longest day of the year? Answer: The 21st of June.

Here is my beautiful garden.

Answer: Early morning or in the evening when the sun is not too hot.

A flower-stand

1. Put pieces of broken pots in the bottom of the stand.
2. Cover with soil.
3. Plant some flowers. Water them.

A FLOWER-POT HOLDER

an old copper kettle

a cast-iron pot

Today is hot!

Before going away on holiday, check that you take all the clothes you need.

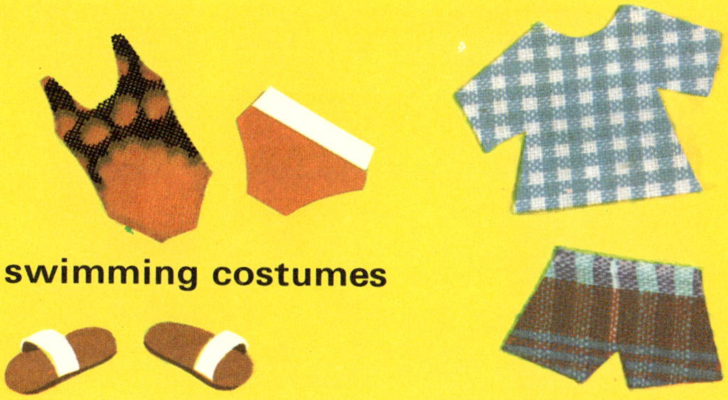

swimming costumes

sandals, light clothing

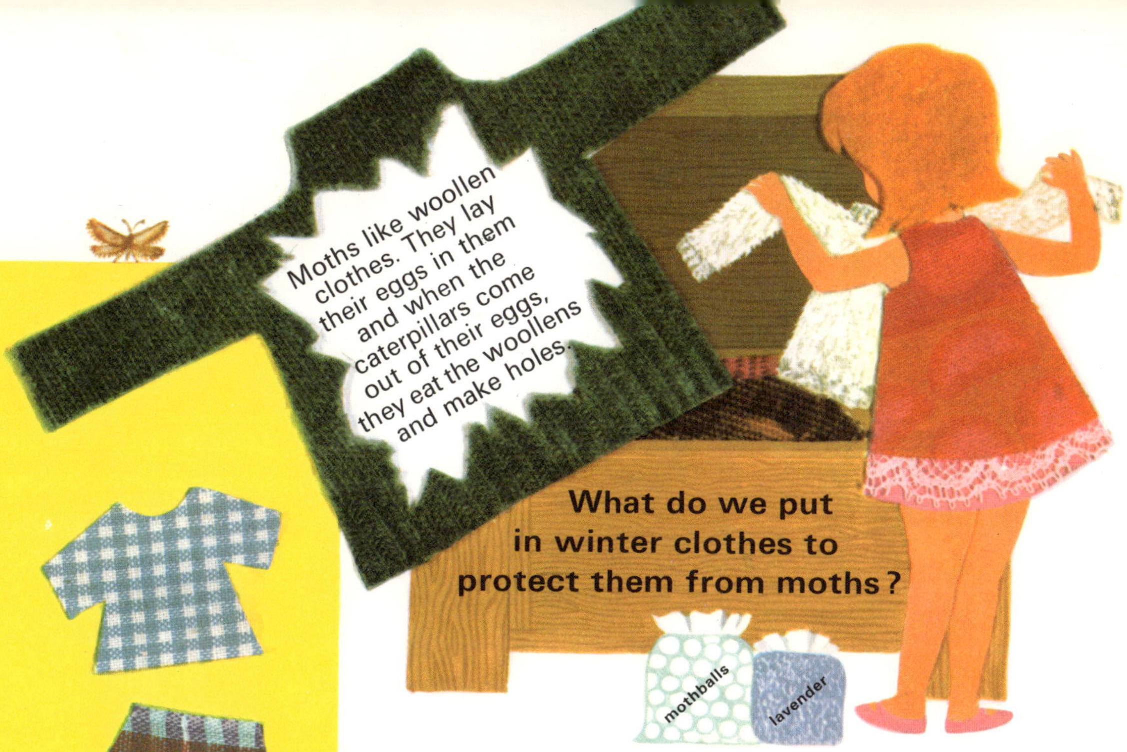
Moths like woollen clothes. They lay their eggs in them and when the caterpillars come out of their eggs, they eat the woollens and make holes.
mothballs
lavender

What do we put in winter clothes to protect them from moths?

Let's pretend . . .

. . . we are living in Africa where it is hot all the time.

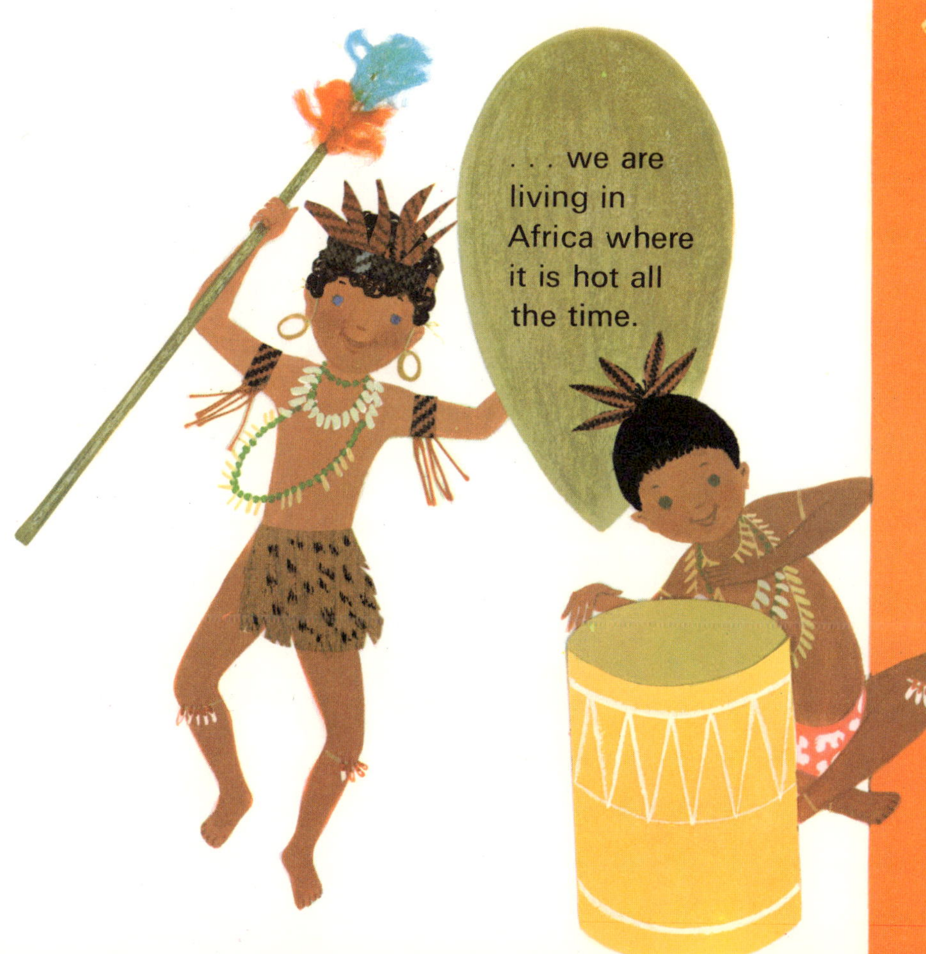

Necklaces

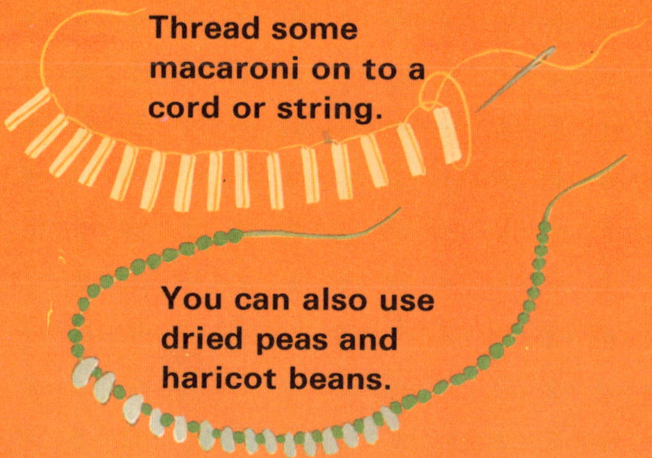

Thread some macaroni on to a cord or string.

You can also use dried peas and haricot beans.

A tom-tom

Make with a circular box covered with paper, painted and decorated.

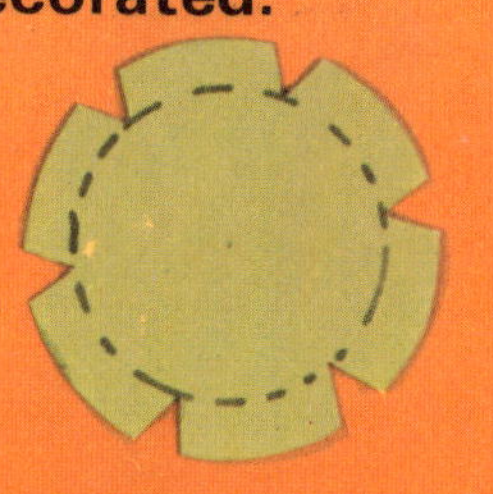

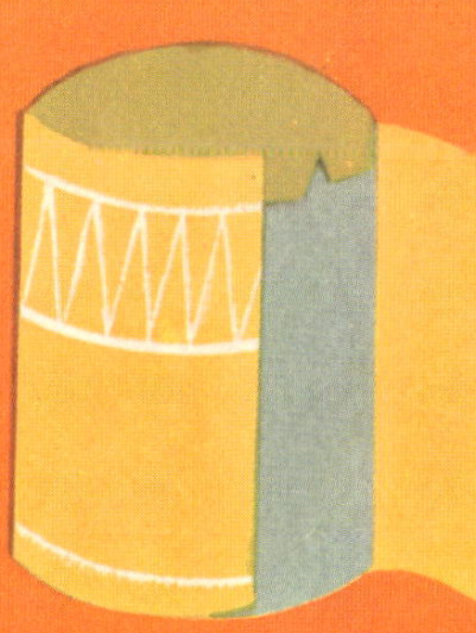

Summer vegetables

Why is it good to eat vegetables?

Spinach is extra good for children because it contains iron as well as vitamins.

Answer: Because they contain vitamins which are absolutely essential to good health!

Strawberries and Cherries

strawberry jam

cherry jam

In summer the red fruits ripen first, and then peaches and apricots.

Do not pick wild berries to to eat – they may be poisonous.

These are soft fruits and are delicious even when cooked and changed into jam and syrup.

hoe

A LANTERN

Cut off the top of a large melon and hollow it out with a spoon. Cut out the eyes and mouth. Make three holes in the top and thread string through to hang. Make another hole in the bottom for the candle.

The sun shines

The beach, the sea, the birds are waiting for you.

THE SAILOR BOY'S ADVICE

LOW TIDE

HIGH TIDE

For several hours, the sea goes out:
this is low tide, when you can pick up the shells left in the sand.
But don't dawdle, for the sea comes back up and covers the shore: this is high tide.

How to make fire with water:

You will need 2 watch-glasses filled with water and joined together with clear tape.
I pencil slit part way down to use for the handle.
Slot the glasses into the pencil slit, hold over some dry moss and focus the sun's rays on the glass.

for everyone.

THE RICHES OF THE SEA

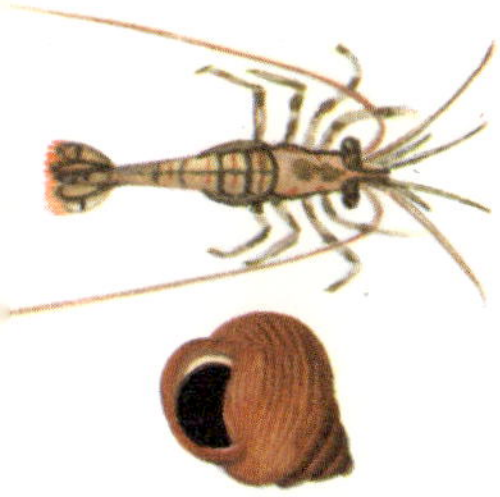

Fish for shrimp with a net, and with a knife cut off the winkle.

PIRATE TREASURE

crab

lobster

WE ARE GOING TO HAVE FUN WITH THESE SHELLS

barnacle cockle mussel clam snail scallop

PEBBLE PAPERWEIGHTS

Paint the larger pebbles and then varnish.

SHELL TRINKETS

A necklace

A tortoise

A barnacle (the shell)
A winkle (the head)
A cockle (the feet)

Summer plants: simple, but nice!

In fields or in the borders of hedgerows, wild plants grow which people pick to use as medicines.

verbascum

camomile

mallow

mint

arnica

PRETTY . . . BUT DANGEROUS

do not pick

Flowers to pick

The scarecrow is a dummy put in the fields to frighten birds which try to eat the seeds.

Harvest-time

The corn is ripe. Big machines cross the fields and harvest the corn. Then it is loaded on to lorries and carried to big tanks called silos. From there, it is sent to mills, which change it into flour.

The combine-harvester cuts the corn and separates the grain from the chaff.

Children gather up the cornflowers and sheafs of corn to make pretty bouquets.

How to make a straw doll

The wood's residents

During the hot season, birds sing the most at dawn and dusk.

FRIENDS OF THE FOREST BEWARE OF FIRE!

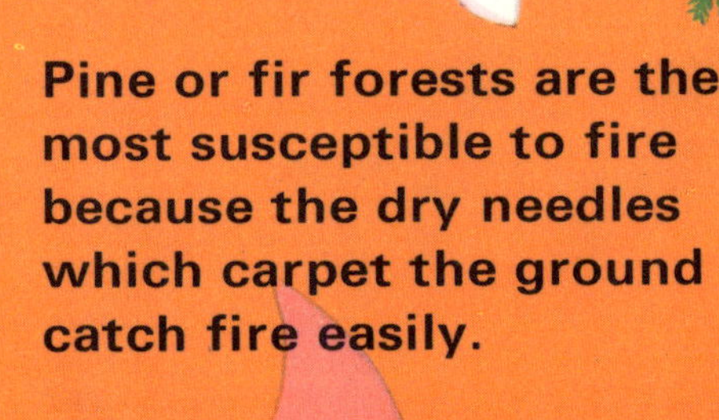

Pine or fir forests are the most susceptible to fire because the dry needles which carpet the ground catch fire easily.

Let's Pretend . . .

WE ARE SIOUX WARRIORS AND MAKE A BOW.

We need a branch of ash, acacia, yew, willow or hazel-tree and

some hemp cord.

Bend the branch and tie the cord at the two ends.

TO MAKE AN INDIAN HEADDRESS:

Cut a long strip of cardboard and shape as in diagram.

Decorate the cardboard. Fix feathers on the back with sticking plaster from the centre of one of the outer edges. Fold the half without feathers over to meet the half with feathers and glue from the tail edge leaving enough space for your head.

DO NOT BREAK ANY BRANCHES

If you want to make a bow, ask a forester to cut you some boughs. He will be able to choose them for you without hurting the trees.

Fox cubs are afraid of fire.

In the mountains

The young eagle has become big and strong. Rabbits, rats and marmots beware . . .

the eagle's home

Mountain flowers grow in dangerous places, so be careful picking them.

Something to make with mountain flowers

Put the flowers between two pieces of blotting paper in a heavy book and leave for several days.

Cut a piece of clear plastic and cardboard the size of the pot. (Leave an extra 1 cm at the edges.)

Lambs caper in the mountains. When winter approaches they move to the lower pastures.

THE WEATHER MAN

Pin an acorn on to a pine cone.

Draw on the eyes and mouth.

Glue two feathers under two scales of the pinecone, and two cocktail sticks which are fixed into a box. When the weather is fair and dry, the scales stand on end, and the man raises his arms. When it rains, the scales close up and his arms move to his body again.

Paste the flowers on to the cardboard. Cover with the clear plastic. Make small holes in the top and bottom. Thread some string through them. Wrap this band around the pot. Secure the ends with clear adhesive tape.

Like a fish in the river

When it's hot, it's good to splash in the cool water.

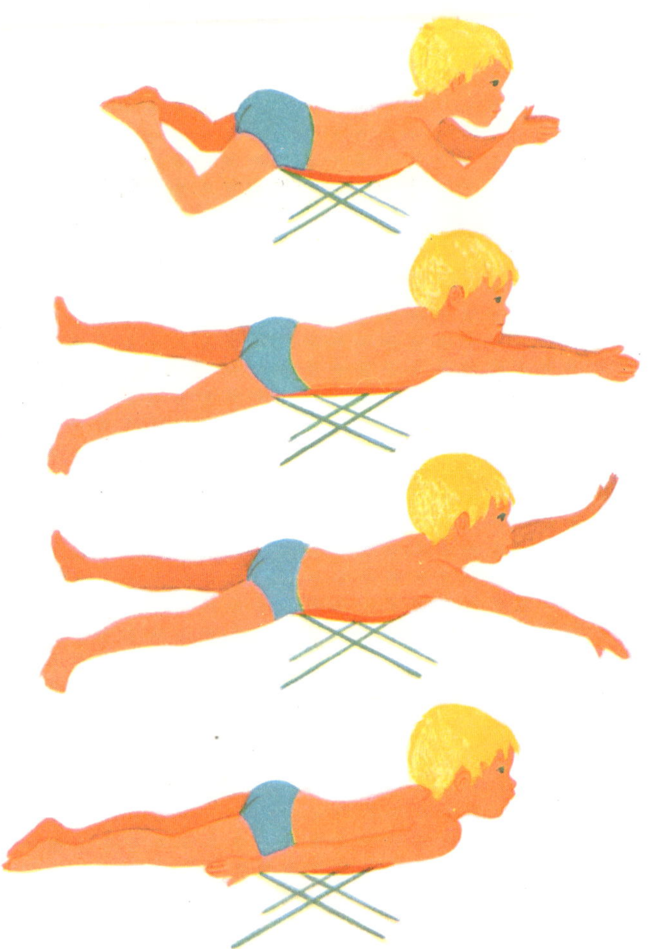

Some exercises to help you learn to swim.

I've been sunbathing and now I'm going for a swim.

But wait! Don't jump into the water if you are too hot! Stay in the shade awhile until you are cooler.

During summer, fish look for their food early in the morning or round about dusk, when it is cooler.

21st September
Autumn has begun!
Take with you

Your Souvenirs of a Lovely Summer . . .

some sheafs of corn, everlasting dried flowers, seaweed and shells, butterflies and stones.

Autumn

I pack my school satchel

my elevenses

an apple

bread and butter

chocolate

jotters

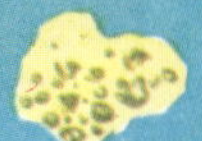

a sponge for cleaning the jotters

a drawing book

coloured pencils

exercise books

a pencil case

I cover my books.

Clothes I wear in the autumn:

a pinafore,
strong walking
shoes,
a sou'wester
and a raincoat
in case
it rains,
and wellingtons
to paddle
through the
muddy streets.

It has been dark by about eight o'clock in the evening ever since the end of September.

Delicious fruits

from the orchard are ready for us to taste!

In autumn apple trees and pear trees are laden with ripe fruit.

Jobs

to do in the garden to make it more beautiful.

Making toys out of walnuts

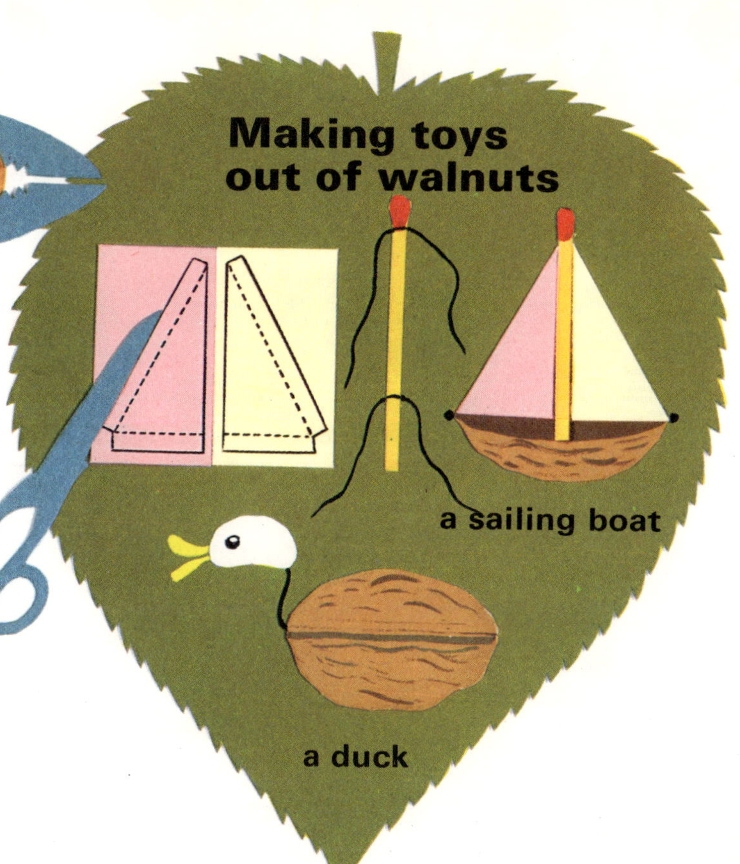

SEPTEMBER

This is the time to plant trees.

OCTOBER

Dead leaves must be raked up.

You can plant onions and tulips now.

NOVEMBER

Marvellous large fires are made to burn all the dead leaves.

Lovely vegetables

In autumn I put on my raincoat when I go shopping at the market.

The last autumn vegetables are picked in October.

cabbages
pimientos
beans
beetroot

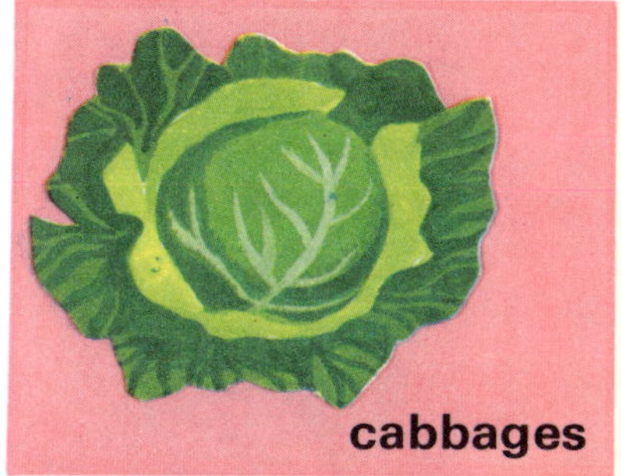

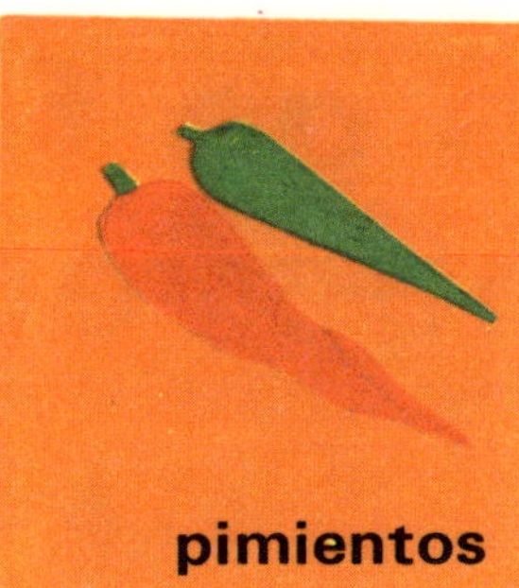

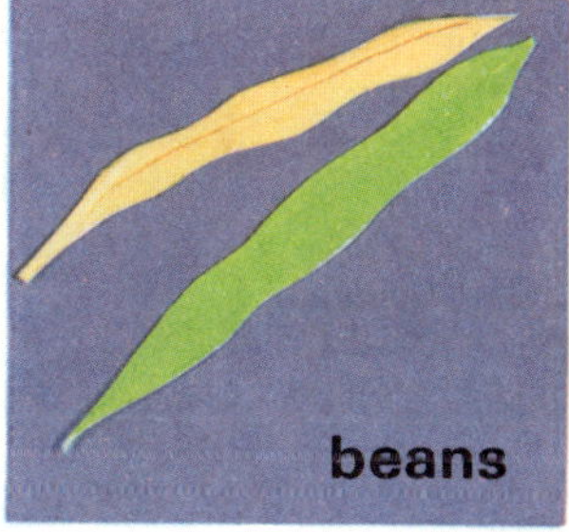

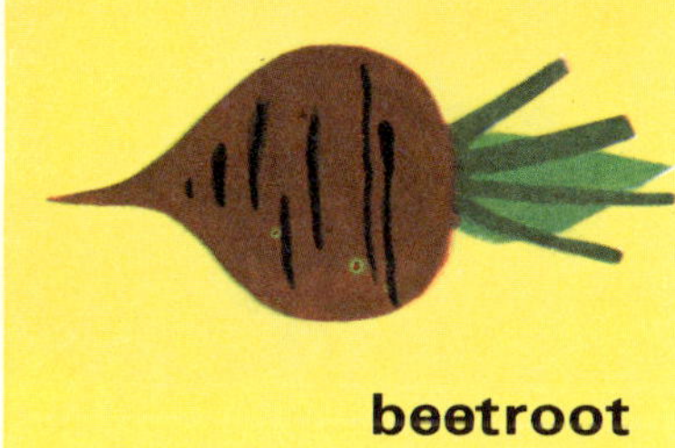

Printing with potatoes

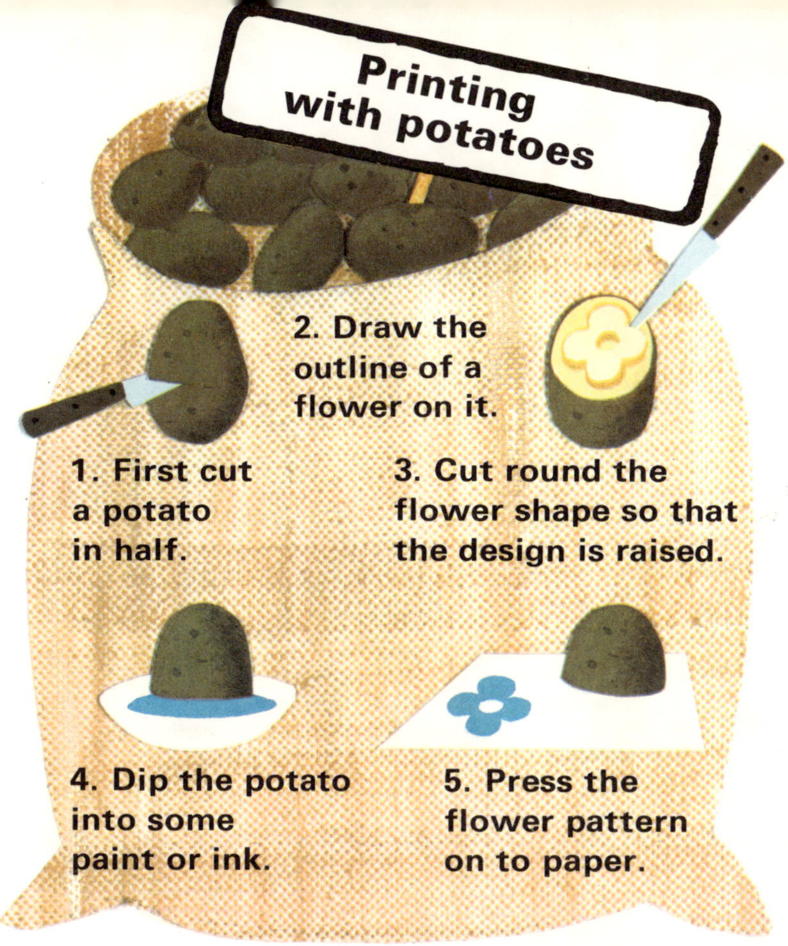

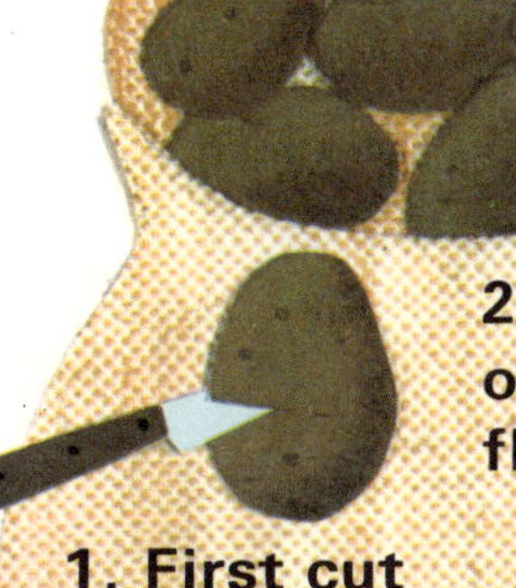

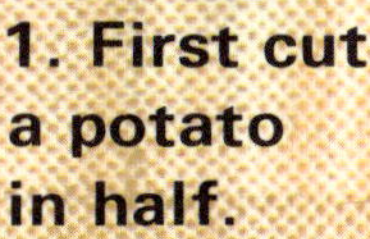

1. First cut a potato in half.

2. Draw the outline of a flower on it.

3. Cut round the flower shape so that the design is raised.

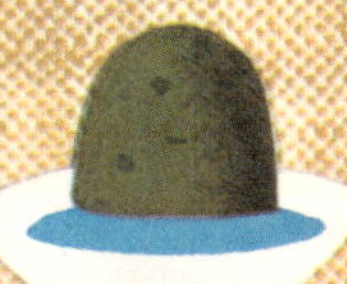

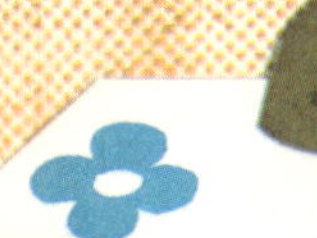

4. Dip the potato into some paint or ink.

5. Press the flower pattern on to paper.

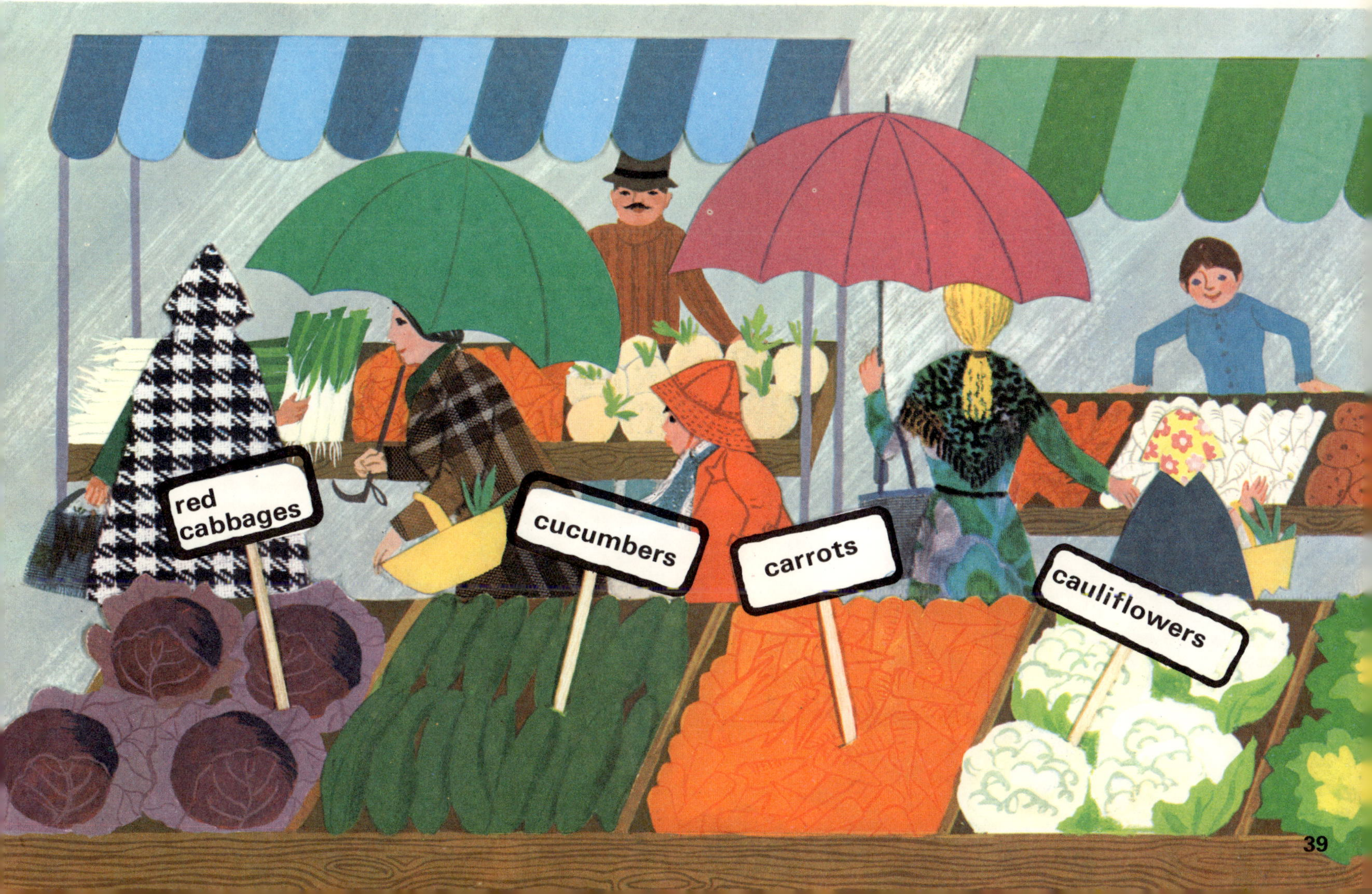

red cabbages
cucumbers
carrots
cauliflowers

Let's go for a walk in the wood

Some thrushes come to Britain during the autumn, and stay here all winter.

Pheasants sleep in trees.

This hunter is on the look-out for game. The children are collecting chestnuts and beautiful red and yellow leaves which have fallen to the ground.

In the wood you will find many different kinds of mushrooms, but they are not all safe to eat.

What fun it is playing with conkers!

Sweet chestnuts are delicious!

hazelnut

acorn

chestnut

A squirrel fills its winter larder with acorns and hazelnuts.

A game to play with . . .

A SYCAMORE KEY

Throw it in the air and watch it turn like a propeller.

AN ACORN

Make the head of a little old man.

A CHESTNUT

You'll have an owl!

Playing in the wind

A propeller

Fold a piece of paper in half. Cut out a shape which looks like a tongue.

Twist one side over and the other side under.

Push a pin, strung with a couple of beads, through the centre, and then stick the pin into a cork.

Now run, and watch the propeller turn round and round!

A weathercock

Cut an arrow from a piece of cardboard.

Stick a pin in the middle of the arrow, and you'll see it pointing in the direction the wind is blowing!

A paper dart

1. Fold a piece of paper in half.

2. Fold back a corner on each side.

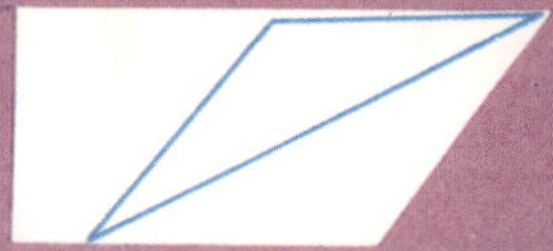

3. Bring the fold up even with the top fold; crease.

4. Do the same on the other side.

5. Again bring the fold up even with the top fold; crease.

6. Then do it again on the other side.

Now turn the dart over . . . and throw it!

A kite

Nail together two strips of plywood, or willow shoots, at right angles and glue paper on to this frame.

Tie a piece of string to the longer stick in two places.

Tie several pieces of coloured paper or ribbon to the tail-string and attach it to the frame. Then let the kite float upwards!

Playing with your toys in front of the fire

How is your house warmed?

A magic merry-go-round

Draw diagonal lines on a square piece of paper.

Beginning at each corner, cut halfway along each of the four lines.

Fold the corners towards the centre, and glue them firmly.

Cut out four small horses, and suspend them from each corner of the merry-go-round.

Hung well above the fire, the horses will go round and round!

In the country

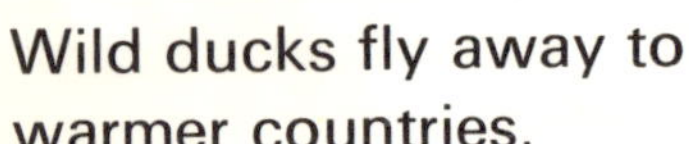

Wild ducks fly away to warmer countries.

In the autumn, storks go to Africa to spend the winter.

Crows don't mind the cold weather so they stay here.

It's fun to grow plants.

Fill the holes of a damp sponge with cress seeds, and place the sponge in a saucer filled with water.

A few days later you will see marvellous results!

Put some damp cottonwool in a saucer. Place lentils on top, making sure the cottonwool remains moist.

A few weeks later beautiful green shoots will appear.

This farmer is ploughing his fields. He turns the soil over and then plants the seeds, which will grow into wheat next summer.

In the city

It is nearly the middle of December now, and the autumn is just about over.
The first snowflakes have started to fall.
'Oh, how very cold it is!' the little sparrows seem to say, as they shiver on a branch.
Everyone is thrilled to see the nice man who sells hot chestnuts again! At any moment winter will be here.
Goodbye, beautiful autumn!

Winter

It only becomes light at about eight o'clock. But gradually the sun rises earlier each day until even the very early morning is light . . .

Which is the shortest day of the year?

. . . and how cold it is! But when the sun shines . . .

The first day of winter!

I have great fun watching my shadow at one o'clock in the afternoon. Ever since the autumn I have watched it, day after day, growing and growing, right up to the 22nd December—when it suddenly stops growing!

How to make paper snowflakes

Cut out a circle. Fold it in half, then in thirds. Cut two zig-zag lines like in the picture on the right. Finally, unfold the paper and see what you have!

At about five o'clock in the afternoon it starts to get dark.

But the days start to grow longer as the sun sets later and later.

22
DECEMBER

Getting ready for cold weather

Eskimos

live in
the polar regions.
To protect themselves
from the cold, they
eat seal blubber, and
feast on . . . cod-liver
oil!

What is happening in hot countries?

The people who live there
are growing:

grapefruit
oranges
lemons

atchoo!

Grapefruit,
oranges and
lemon juice
are all very
good for us
because they
are full of
something
called vitamin C,
which helps to
prevent us from
catching colds.

Before going outside you must dress yourself properly.

Put on:

a hat,

an overcoat,

boots,

and warm gloves.

CROCHETING WITH WOOL

When you've learned to crochet, you can make a woolly hat!

Fun and games

Whose footprints are these?

for winter holidays

Twist the fuse wire round the silver wire. Wind this round a glass. Let it slide off and place the spiral flat on a table. Arrange the centre in a coil again, and tie as shown.

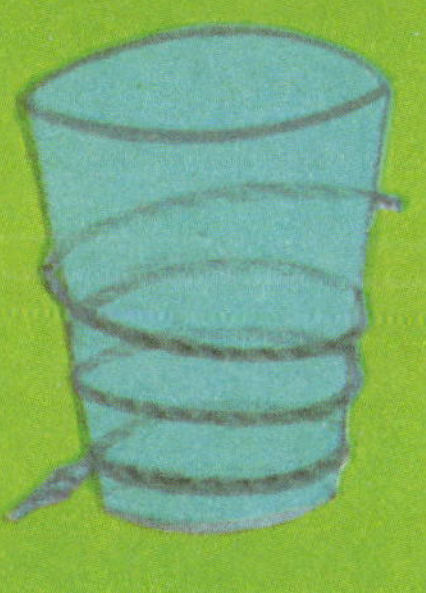

How to make Spirals

The Three Wise Men

Paint the faces, glue on the cottonwool beard and dress the pinecones in gay cloaks.

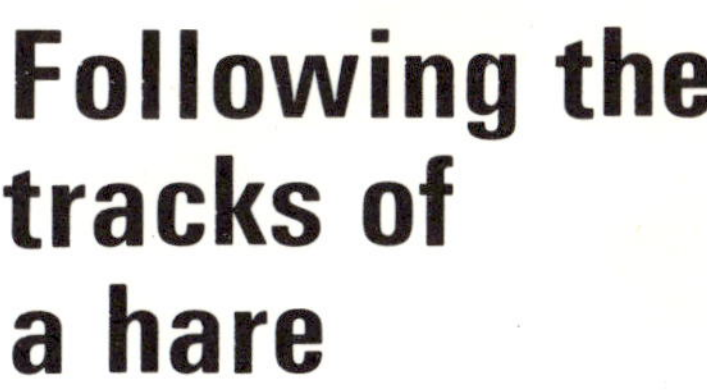

Following the tracks of a hare

A hare bounds along in a straight line, and his back feet are longer than his front ones. From the prints he leaves in the snow, it looks as if the hare's back feet land in front of his front feet!

Happy Christmas!

An angel

Cut half a circle out of white cardboard and make it into the shape of a cone. Glue the edges together so that it can stand.

Draw the angel's head and wings on another piece of cardboard and cut the shape out.

Glue yellow wool or thread on to the head as hair. Cut out a star from either gold or silver paper and attach it to the back of the angel's head.

A cableway

Start with a long piece of nylon cord and two large nails: knock one in near the ceiling and the other nearly at floor level on the opposite wall, and put a cotton reel on each. Tie the nylon cord round the reels and attach the angels to the cord. Then gently pull . . .

. . . and the angels will rise!

Paper chains

1. Place strips of paper on top of each other at right angles.
2. Glue strip A round strip B, and then B round A, making sure they are strongly linked. Keep adding strips until the chain is long enough.

The Ice Palace

It is freezing. You have accidentally left a bottle full of water outside.

Next day you find it has cracked open. Why?

The water froze because of the cold. Ice takes up more room than water, and so the bottle broke when the water changed to ice.

JANUARY

Be careful! Icicles aren't sugar lumps!

CELEBRATING TWELFTH NIGHT

Green frogs hibernate in the mud on the bottom of streams or ponds.

A TWELFTH NIGHT CAKE

This celebration takes place in January, and it is in honour of the Three Wise Men. While you are making the cake you must hide a tiny doll in it. The person who finds the doll in his slice becomes 'king'. He chooses his queen, and the two of them are crowned.

Formerly a real bean was baked in the Twelfth-night cake, but nowadays it has been replaced by a tiny doll.

When you slip or slide, throw yourself forward and try to avoid falling!

Carp and tench spend the winter only half awake.

A crown

Trace the outline of this crown.
Copy the shape on to yellow- or gold-coloured cardboard, and cut it out. Stick on coloured pieces of paper that look like jewels. Glue the ends of the crown together, and it is ready to wear!

the shortest month of the year

At last the weather is becoming milder. The snow melts, rushing down the mountain sides. This is called an avalanche!

Grouse are still wearing their winter coats of white. When spring comes, however, their feathers will turn brown.

Forests should not be destroyed. They often prevent avalanches from damaging houses and farms.

Tortoises awake from their long winter sleep.

February is just about over!

How many days are there in February?

28 days—but every fourth year, 29!

Let's dress up!

The little Martian

Cut a rectangle out of thin cardboard for the head. In the middle of it cut out eyes and a mouth. Using tape, join the ends to make a cylinder.

Cut out a circle as shown on the right and place it over the cylinder. Stick a pencil in the middle and wind some fuse wire or string round it.

To make the arms, cut out 4 rectangles, making them into 4 cylinders. Tie 2 together at a single point; do same for the other pair.

For the breastplate, cut another rectangle out of cardboard, the measurement of your chest.

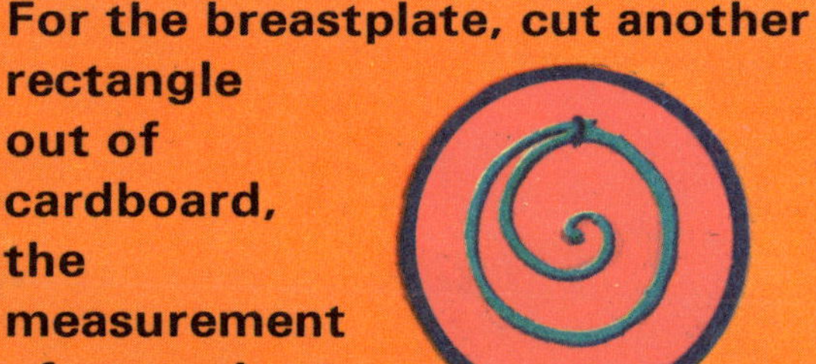

Cut 2 long strips of cardboard to make straps. Make slots in the breastplate, and pass the straps through them, fixing with tape. Now try it all on!

Glue a paper circle in the centre, outlined with flex or string, which should also be glued on. Join the ends of the rectangle together with tape, to make a cylinder.

chestnuts

Seeds fall to the ground in the autumn, and during the winter are protected from the cold by a blanket of snow.

During the winter the forest goes to sleep.

Many animals hibernate—that is, they sleep through the entire winter.

What do bears do?
Bears wake up from time to time, prowl around for awhile, and then go back to sleep.

DORMICE
sleep until spring in the hollows of trees or in abandoned nests.

HEDGEHOGS
hibernate under rocks or between the roots of trees, making lairs lined with leaves and moss.

What about ADDERS?
They don't move at all—they remain safely hidden in a hole somewhere!

MARCH

Take off your heavy winter coats!

Look at the pretty snowdrop!  Spring is nearly here.

The snow melts. The sun shines more strongly, warming the earth. Lovely spring is here again!